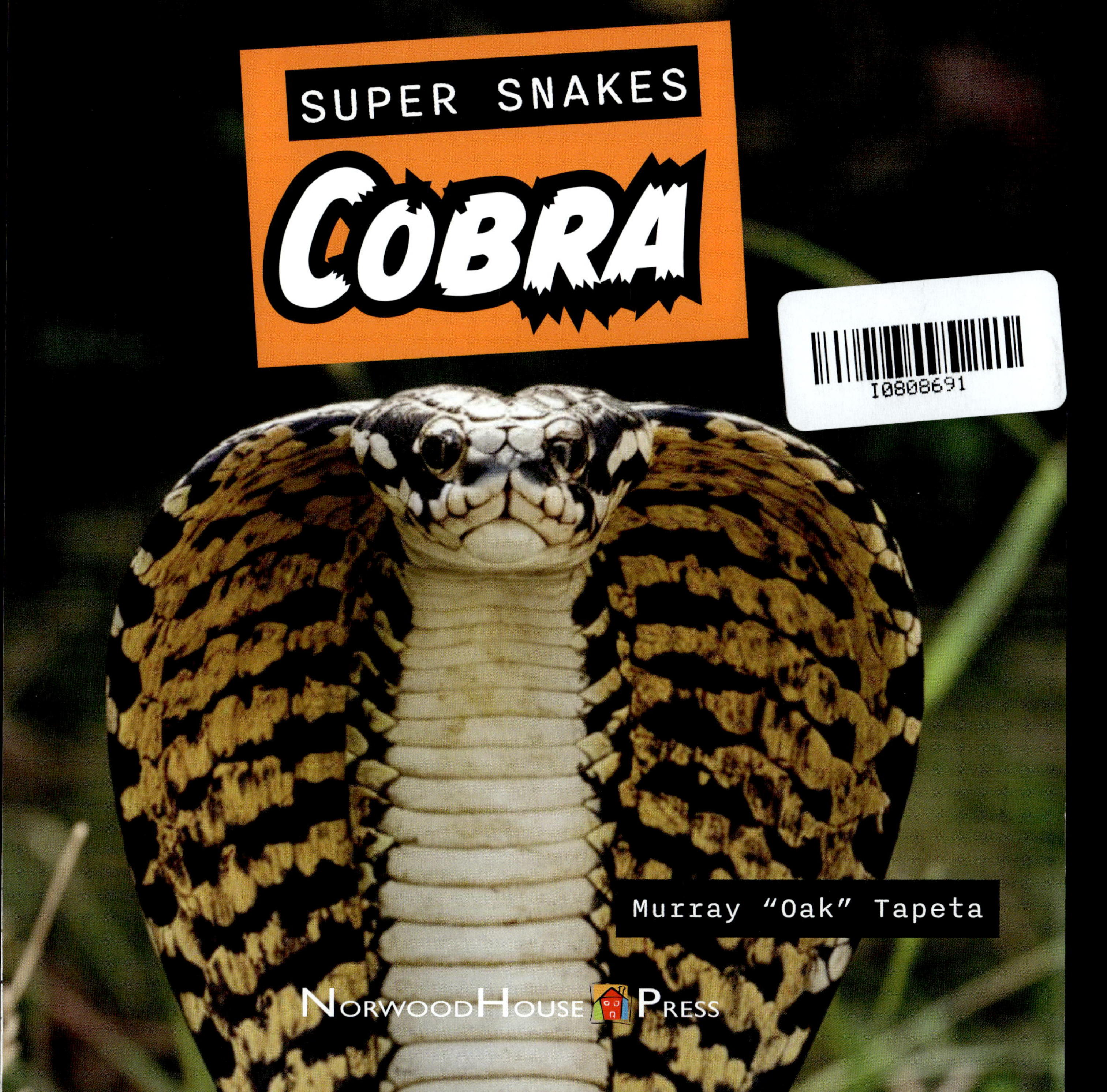

SUPER SNAKES

COBRA

Murray "Oak" Tapeta

NorwoodHouse Press

Cataloging-in-Publication Data

Names: Tapeta, Murray.
Title: Cobra / Murray Tapeta.
Description: Buffalo, NY : Norwood House Press, 2026. | Series: Super snakes | Includes glossary and index.
Identifiers: ISBN 9781978575073 (pbk.) | ISBN 9781978575080 (library bound) | ISBN 9781978575097 (ebook)
Subjects: LCSH: Cobras--Juvenile literature. | King cobra--Juvenile literature.
Classification: LCC QL666.O64 T374 2026 | DDC 597.96'42--dc23

Published in 2026 by
Norwood House Press
2544 Clinton Street
Buffalo, NY 14224

Designer: Rhea Magaro
Editor: Kim Thompson

Photo credits: Cover, p. 1, 5 Dream Frame Photography /Shutterstock.com; p. 3 Photo Nature Travel /Shutterstock.com; p. 6 Photography Phor Phun /Shutterstock.com; p. 7 sagarkhunte /Shutterstock.com; pp. 8, 9 Isroi /Shutterstock.com; p. 10 Vova Shevchuk /Shutterstock.com; p. 11 Robert Wedderburn /Shutterstock.com; p. 12 Kurit afshen / Shutterstock.com; p. 13 Reto Buehler /Shutterstock.com; p. 14 stalk /Shutterstock.com; p. 15 Anton_Ivanov /Shutterstock.com; p. 16 Cormac Price /Shutterstock.com; p. 19 Riadi Pracipta66 /Shutterstock.com; p. 20 Ton Bangkeaw /Shutterstock.com; p. 21 Tongsai /Shutterstock.com;

Printed in the United States of America

TABLE OF CONTENTS

What Is Special about Cobras?

Cobras are some of the largest poisonous snakes in the world. When a cobra feels threatened, it tries to look even bigger! It raises the top part of its body. Its neck flares out into a **hood**. It makes a loud hiss.

What Do Cobras Look Like?

There are more than 20 different cobra **species**. Cobras can be black, brown, green, yellow, and red.

Some cobras have **markings**. The Indian cobra has two circles on the back of its hood. The snake looks like it is wearing glasses!

Cobras are long and thin. King cobras are the longest. They can grow 19 feet (six meters) long!

A king cobra can lift the top third of its body off the ground. This helps it see over tall grass.

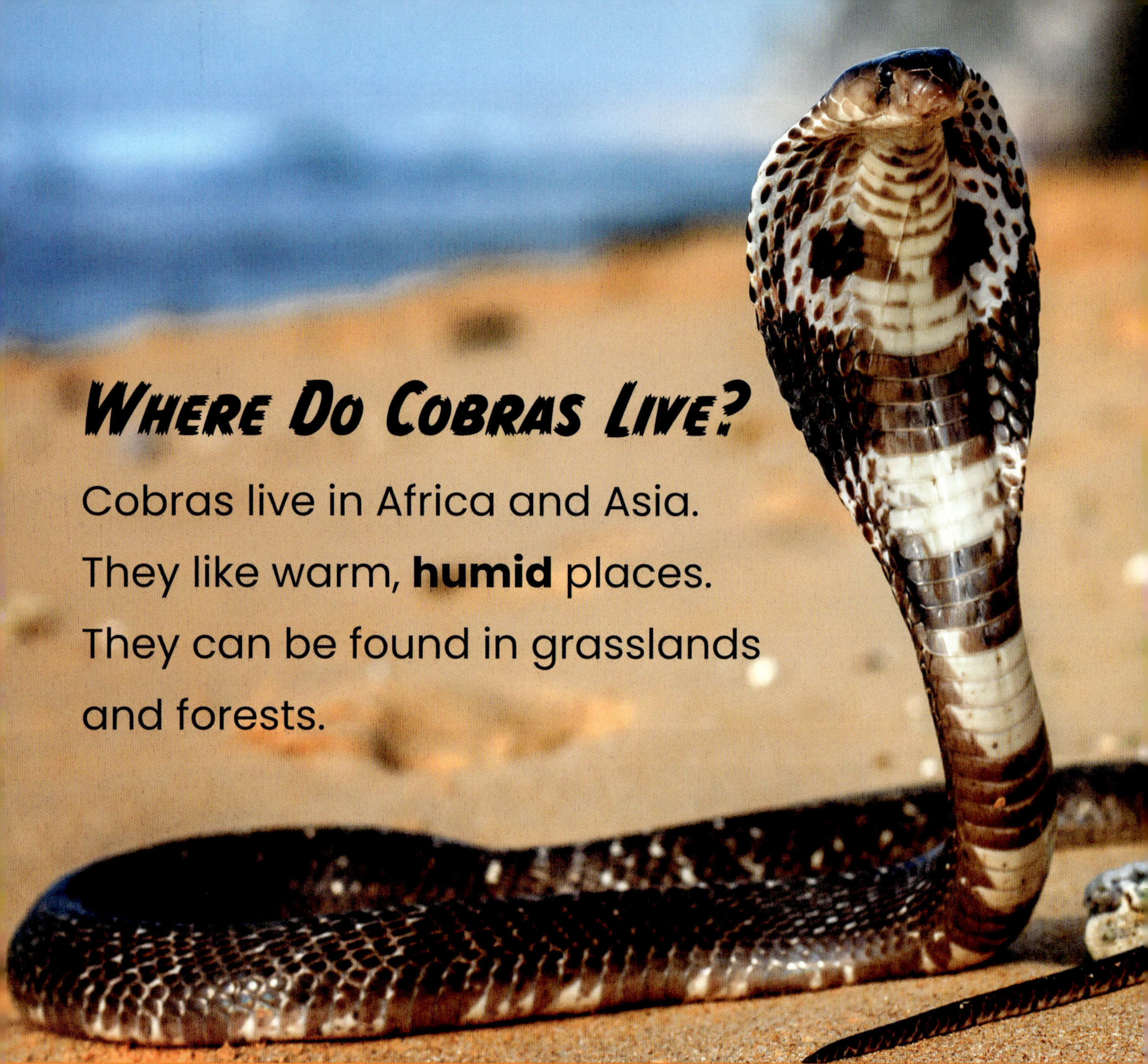

Where Do Cobras Live?

Cobras live in Africa and Asia. They like warm, **humid** places. They can be found in grasslands and forests.

King cobras look for forests near streams. They spend about one-quarter of their lives up in trees!

How Do Cobras Hunt?

A cobra can wait weeks between meals. Hungry cobras hunt at dawn and dusk. Their **forked** tongues taste the air to track their prey.

Cobras look for mice, rats, and rabbits. They also eat **amphibians**, birds, lizards, eggs, and even other snakes!

Cobras strike with **fangs** that inject a dose of **venom**. The venom stuns the victim and stops its heart. The Egyptian cobra's venom is extra **toxic**. It brings a quick death.

Cobras only attack people to protect themselves or their eggs. A cobra bite can kill a human. King cobras carry enough venom to kill an elephant!

Some cobras seem to spit their venom. They do not really spit. They squeeze muscles to make venom spray out of their fangs.

The **mongoose** is quick enough and brave enough to hunt cobras. It darts in and bites the cobra's neck.

How Do Cobras Reproduce?

A female cobra lays eggs each year. She guards them until they hatch. Babies care for themselves as soon as they are born.

A king cobra mother is extra careful. She builds a nest from leaves. She curls up on the nest to keep the eggs warm until they hatch.

Glossary

amphibians (am-FIB-ee-uhnz): cold-blooded animals with backbones that live both in water and on land, such as frogs, toads, and salamanders

fangs (fangz): long, pointed teeth

forked (forkd): divided into two branches or points

hood (hud): an expansion of the body that looks like a covering for the head

humid (HYOO-mid): moist and hot

markings (MAHRK-ingz): colored lines, shapes, or patterns on the surface of something

mongoose (MAHN-goos): a mammal with a slender body, long tail, and brown or black fur

species (SPEE-seez): a group of similar living things that can reproduce with each other

toxic (TAHK-sik): poisonous

venom (VEN-uhm): a toxic substance that is produced by an animal to harm or kill prey and enemies

Thinking Questions

1. On what continents do cobras live?
2. When does a cobra have a hood?
3. What do cobras eat?
4. How does a cobra use its tongue?
5. How often do cobras lay eggs?

Index

About the Author

Murray "Oak" Tapeta was born in a cabin without plumbing in Montana. Growing up in the great outdoors, he became a lover of nature. He earned the nickname "Oak" after climbing to the top of an oak tree at the age of three. Oak loves to read and write. He has written many books about events in history and other subjects that fascinate him. He prefers spending time in the wilderness with his dog Birchy.